Soprano

W9-BWD-903

THE SINGERS MUSICAL THEATRE ANTHOLOGY

A collection of songs from the musical stage, categorized by voice type. The selections are presented in their authentic settings, excerpted from the original vocal scores.

Hal Leonard Publishing Corporation

ISBN 0-88188-546-0

7777 West Bluemound Road
P.O. Box 13819 Milwaukee, WI 53213

Foreword

The Singer's Musical Theatre Anthology is the most comprehensive series of its kind ever to appear in print. Its unique perspective is in looking at the field of musical theatre in terms of vocal literature. One of the prime parameters in choosing the songs for this series was that they should all be, in some way, particularly vocally gratifying.

Many of the songs included here are very familiar to us, yet we seldom see them printed as they were originally written and performed. The long tradition in sheet music throughout this century has been to adapt a song in several ways to conform to a format which makes it accessible to the average pianist. This type of arrangement is what one finds in vocal selections, or in any piano/vocal collection of show music. These sheet arrangements serve their purpose very well, but aren't really the best performing editions for a singer. In contrast, the selections in this series have been excerpted from the original vocal scores. One of the many benefits of this is a much more satisfying piano accompaniment. In addition, many songs included here have never been available separately from the full vocal scores.

In some cases, a song has required some adaptation in order to be excerpted from a show's vocal score. The practice of performing arias as removed from their operatic context gives many precedents for making such adjustments. In many ways, one could view this anthology as a "critical edition," or a "performing edition." Significant editorial adjustments are indicated by footnotes in some instances.

The original keys of this literature (which are used here) can give important information to a singer about the nature of a song and how it should sound, and in most cases they will work very well for most singers. But unlike opera, these original keys do not necessarily need to be reverently maintained. With some musical theatre literature, a singer should not rule out transposing a song up or down for vocal comfortability. Mezzo-sopranos in particular may find some of their songs in inaccessibly low keys and may need to transpose them up. Concerning keys, one important factor to remember is that the preferred vocal sound in women's musical theatre literature is often significantly lower than as defined by classical vocal tradition, especially by operatic standards of tessitura.

There is certainly no codified system for classifying theatre music as to voice type. With some roles the classification is obvious. With others there is a good deal of ambiguity. As a result, a particular singer might find suitable literature in this anthology in both volumes of his/her gender. Specifically, a classically trained mezzo-soprano will find many comfortable songs in the soprano volume.

Any performer of these songs will benefit greatly by a careful study of the show and role from which any given song is taken. This type of approach is taken for granted with an actor preparing a monologue or an opera singer preparing an aria. But because much theatre music has been the popular music of its time, we sometimes easily lose awareness of its dramatic context.

The selections in **The Singer's Musical Theatre Anthology** will certainly be significant additions to a singer's repertory, but no anthology can include every wonderful song. There is a vast body of literature, some of it virtually unknown, waiting to be discovered and brought to life.

I would like to thank the following persons for their help in assembling materials for this series: Judy Bell of The Richmond Organization, Paul McKibbins of Tommy Valando Publications, and Lys Symonette of the Kurt Weill Foundation for Music, Inc.

Richard Walters, editor

THE SINGER'S MUSICAL THEATRE ANTHOLOGY
Soprano

Contents

About The Shows

ALLEGRO

MUSIC: Richard Rodgers
LYRICS AND BOOK: Oscar Hammerstein II
DIRECTOR AND CHOREOGRAPHER: Agnes de Mille
OPENED: 10/10/47

Allegro was the third Rodgers and Hammerstein musical on Broadway and the first with a story that had not been based on a previous source. It was a particularly ambitious undertaking, with its theme of the corrupting effect of big institutions told through the life of a doctor, Joseph Taylor, Jr. (John Battles), from his birth in a small American town to his thirty-fifth year. Joe grows up, goes to school, marries a local belle (Roberta Jonay), joins the staff of a large Chicago hospital that panders to wealthy patients, discovers that his wife is unfaithful, and, in the end, returns to his home town with his adoring nurse (Lisa Kirk) to dedicate himself to healing the sick and helping the needy. One innovation in the musical was the use of a Greek chorus to comment on the action and to sing directly to the actors and the audience.

BABES IN ARMS

MUSIC: Richard Rodgers
LYRICS: Lorenz Hart
DIRECTOR: Robert Sinclair
OPENED: 4/14/37

BOOK: Richard Rodgers and Lorenz Hart
CHOREOGRAPHER: George Balanchine

With such songs as "I Wish I Were In Love Again," "Johnny One Note," "The Lady Is A Tramp," "My Funny Valentine," and "Where Or When," *Babes In Arms* boasted more hits than any of Rodgers and Hart's twenty-nine stage musicals. In the high-spirited, youthful show, a group of youngsters, whose parents are out-of-work vaudevillians, stage a revue to keep from being sent to a work farm. Unfortunately, the show is not a success. Later, when a transatlantic French flyer lands nearby, they attract enough publicity to put on a successful show and have their own youth center. Among the cast's babes in arms were such future stars as Alfred Drake and Dan Dailey, both appearing in their first Broadway roles.

MGM's 1939 film version, starring Mickey Rooney and Judy Garland, retained only two of the Rodgers and Hart songs. The director was Busby Berkeley.

THE BOYS FROM SYRACUSE

MUSIC: Richard Rodgers
LYRICS: Lorenz Hart
DIRECTOR: George Abbott
OPENED: 11/23/38

BOOK: George Abbott
CHOREOGRAPHER: George Balanchine

The idea for *The Boys From Syracuse* began when Rodgers and Hart, while working on another show, were discussing the fact that no one had yet done a musical based on a play by Shakespeare. Their obvious choice was *The Comedy Of Errors* chiefly because Lorenz Hart's brother Teddy Hart was always being confused with another comic actor, Jimmy Savo. Set in Ephesus in ancient Asia Minor, the ribald tale concerns the efforts of two boys from Syracuse, Antipholus and his servant Dromio (Eddie Albert and Jimmy Savo) to find their long-lost twins, also named Antipholus and Dromio (Ronald Graham and Teddy Hart). Complications arise when the wives of the Ephesians, Adriana (Muriel Angelus) and her servant Luce (Wynn Murray), mistake the two strangers for their husbands. A highly successful Off Broadway revival of *The Boys From Syracuse* was presented in 1963 and ran for 502 performances. The movie version, which RKO-Radio released in 1940, starred Allan Jones and Joe Penner (both in dual roles). It was directed by A. Edward Sutherland.

CAMELOT

MUSIC: Frederick Loewe
LYRICS AND BOOK: Alan Jay Lerner
DIRECTOR: Moss Hart
OPENED: 12/3/60

CHOREOGRAPHER: Hanya Holm

Lerner and Loewe's first Broadway production following their spectacular hit, *My Fair Lady,* was another musical based on a highly esteemed work of British fiction, T.H. White's novel, The Once And Future King. Again, too, they were joined by fair lady Julie Andrews and director Moss Hart for an opulently mounted retelling of the Arthurian legend, with its high-minded knights of the round table and its tragic romantic triangle involving King Arthur, his queen Guenevere, and his trusted knight, Sir Lancelot. Helped by a huge advance ticket sale, *Camelot* easily surmounted a divided press to become something of a Broadway legend itself.

In 1980, during a tour headed by Richard Burton, the original King Arthur, *Camelot* returned to New York to play the New York State Theatre for 56 performances. After Burton was succeeded on the road by Richard Harris, the musical came back again, this time to the Winter Garden for an additional 48 performances. Mr. Harris also starred in the film version with Vanessa Redgrave, which Joshua Logan directed for Warner Bros. in 1967.

Most of the material in this section was previously published in **The Broadway Fake Book,** *for which noted author Stanley Green was consultant and contributor.*

CAROUSEL

MUSIC: Richard Rodgers
LYRICS AND BOOK: Oscar Hammerstein II
DIRECTOR: Rouben Mamoulian
OPENED: 4/19/45

CHOREOGRAPHER: Agnes de Mille

The collaborators of *Oklahoma!* chose Ferenc Molnar's *Liliom* as the basis for their second show. Oscar Hammerstein shifted Molnar's Budapest locale to a late nineteenth century fishing village in New England. The two principal roles are Billy Bigelow, a shiftless carnival barker, and Julie Jordan, an ordinary factory worker. This is not merely a simple boy meets girl plot, but contains a predominant theme of tragedy throughout most of the play. The score is rich with musical high points, the first coming with "If I Loved You," sung by Julie and Billy at their first meeting. In "Mister Snow" Carrie, Julie's friend, describes her almost perfect fiance. Billy's famous "Soliloquy" is Richard Rodgers longest and most operatic song, and can truly be considered an aria. The show closes with the moving, hymn-like "You'll Never Walk Alone."

CELEBRATION

MUSIC: Harvey Schmidt
LYRICS AND BOOK: Tom Jones
DIRECTOR: Tom Jones
OPENED: 1/22/69

The setting is New Year's Eve, that most hopeful of holidays; the theme is of personal renewal and growth. Typically, using a minimum of characters, Schmidt and Jones tell their story with moving simplicity. The song chosen for this anthology, "Under The Tree," is written for a solo singer with a trio, but has been adapted for one singer in the edition that appears here.

FANNY

MUSIC AND LYRICS: Harold Rome
DIRECTOR: Joshua Logan
OPENED: 11/4/54

BOOK: S.N. Behrman and Joshua Logan
CHOREOGRAPHER: Helen Tamiris

Marcel Pagnol's French film trilogy, *Marius, Fanny,* and *Cesar* were combined into one tale as the basis for *Fanny,* the musical. Marseilles is the setting for the intricate plot. It is a soaring, emotional score, well tailored for the talents of a performer such as Ezio Pinza, an opera star who headed the original cast. A film version of the Broadway *Fanny* was made in 1960, starring Leslie Caron, Maurice Chevalier and Charles Boyer, however no songs from the musical were included.

THE FANTASTICKS

MUSIC: Harvey Schmidt
LYRICS AND BOOK: Tom Jones
DIRECTOR: Word Baker
OPENED: 5/3/60

The statistics alone are, well, fantastic. Since *The Fantasticks* opened over twenty-five years ago at a tiny Greenwich Village theatre, there have been, to date, 8,228 productions in the United States, fifteen touring companies, 453 productions in 66 foreign countries, and the backers have received a 7,624% profit on their initial investment of $16,500. No other production, on or off Broadway, has ever enjoyed such a lengthy run. Curiously, the initial reviews were either mixed or negative, and producer Lore Noto seriously considered closing the show after its first discouraging week. But an Off Broadway award, the popularity of the song "Try To Remember," and, most important, word of mouth, all helped to turn the show's fortunes around.

The fragile fantasy is concerned with the theme of seasonal rebirth, or the paradox of "why Spring is born out of Winter's laboring pain." In the story, adapted from Edmond Rostand's play, *Les Ramanesques,* the fathers of two youthful lovers, Luisa and Matt, feel they must show parental disapproval to make sure that their progenies remain together. When this deception is revealed, the lovers quarrel and Matt goes off to seek adventure. At the end, after a number of degrading experiences, he returns to Luisa's waiting arms.

FIDDLER ON THE ROOF

MUSIC: Jerry Bock
LYRICS: Sheldon Harnick
DIRECTOR AND CHOREOGRAPHER: Jerome Robbins
OPENED: 9/22/64

BOOK: Joseph Stein

An undeniable classic of the Broadway theatre, *Fiddler On The Roof* took a compassionate view of a Jewish community in Czarist Russia where the people struggled to maintain their traditions and identity in the face of persecution. Despite a story that some thought had limited appeal (it was based on tales by Sholom Alei-chem, including "Tevye's Daughters"), the theme struck such a universal response that the Fiddler was perched precariously on his roof for a record run of over seven years, nine months. The plot is set in the village of Anatevka in 1905, and deals mainly with the efforts of Tevye (Zero Mostel), a dairyman, his wife Golde (Maria Karnilova), and their five daughters to cope with their harsh existence. At the play's end, when a Cossack pogrom has forced everyone out of the village, Tevye and what is left of his family look forward to a new life in America.

Because of the musical's lengthy run, Zero Mostel was succeeded after a year by Luther Adler, followed by Herschel Bernardi, Harry Goz, Paul Lipson, and Jan Peerce. Others who took over roles during the Broadway engagement were Pia Zadora and Bette Midler, playing two of the daughters. *Fiddler On The Roof* was re-vived on Broadway at the Winter Garden in 1976, with Zero Mostel again in the lead, and at the New York State Theatre in 1981 with Herschel Bernardi and Maria Karnilova.

The United Artists film version, directed by Norman Jewison, opened in 1971 with Topol (who had played Tevye in London), Norma Crane and Molly Picon. Isaac Stern was the violin soloist heard on the soundtrack.

FLOWER DRUM SONG

MUSIC: Richard Rodgers
LYRICS: Oscar Hammerstein II
DIRECTOR: Gene Kelly
OPENED: 12/1/58

BOOK: Oscar Hammerstein II and Joseph Fields
CHOREOGRAPHER: Carol Haney

It was librettist Joseph Fields who first secured the rights to C.Y. Lee's novel and then approached Rodgers and Hammerstein to join him as collaborators. To dramatize the conflict between the traditionalist older Chinese-Americans living in San Francisco and their thoroughly Americanized offsprings, the musical tells the story of Mei Li (Miyoshi Umeki), a timid "picture bride" from China, who arrives to fulfill her contract to marry night-club owner Sammy Fong (Larry Blyden). Sammy, however, prefers dancer Linda Low (Pat Suzuki), who obviously enjoys being a girl, and the problem is resolved when Sammy's friend Wang Ta (Ed Kenney) discovers that Mei Li is really the bride for him. *Flower Drum Song* marked the only Broadway musi-cal directed by Gene Kelly.

In Universal's 1961 movie version, the cast was headed by Miyoshi Umeki, Nancy Kwan, and James Shigeta. Henry Koster was the director.

FOLLIES

MUSIC AND LYRICS: Stephen Sondheim
DIRECTORS: Harold Prince and Michael Bennett
OPENED: 4/4/71

BOOK: James Goldman
CHOREOGRAPHER: Michael Bennett

Taking place at a reunion of former *Ziegfeld Follies*-type showgirls, the musical dealt with the reality of life as contrasted with the unreality of the theatre, a theme it explored through the lives of two couples, the up-per-class, unhappy Phyllis and Benjamin Stone (Alexis Smith and John McMartin) and the middle-class, un-happy Sally and Buddy Plummer (Dorothy Collins and Gene Nelson). *Follies* also depicted these couples as they were in their youth, a flashback device that prompted Stephen Sondheim to come up with songs pur-posely reminiscent of the styles of some of the theatre's great composers and lyricists of the past.

The show was given 2 concert performances in September of 1985 at Avery Fisher Hall in New York City, with a cast that included Barbara Cook, George Hearn, Mandy Patinkin, Lee Remick, Carol Burnett and many oth-ers. A new recording of the musical was released as a result of these performances.

A FUNNY THING HAPPENED ON THE WAY TO THE FORUM

MUSIC AND LYRICS: Stephen Sondheim   **BOOK:** Burt Shevelove and Larry Gelbart
DIRECTOR: George Abbott   **CHOREOGRAPHER:** Jack Cole
OPENED: 5/8/62

Full of sight gags, pratfalls, mistaken identity, leggy girls, and other familiar vaudeville ingredients, this was a bawdy, farcical, pellmell musical whose likes have seldom been seen on Broadway. Originally intended as a vehicle first for Phil Silvers and then for Milton Berle, *A Funny Thing Happened On The Way To The Forum* opened on Broadway with Zero Mostel as Pseudolus the slave, who is forced to go through a series of madcap adventures before being allowed his freedom. Though the show was a hit, things had not looked very promising during the pre-Broadway tryout, and director Jerome Robbins was called in. The most important change: beginning the musical with the song "Comedy Tonight," which set the right mood for the wacky doings that followed.

To come up with a script, the librettists researched all twenty-one surviving comedies by the Roman playwright Plautus (254 BC - 184 BC), then wrote an original book incorporating such typical Plautus characters as the conniving servants, the lascivious master, the domineering mistress, the officious warrior, the simpleminded hero (called Hero), and the senile old man. One situation, regarding the senile old man who is kept from entering his house because he believes it haunted, was, in truth, originally discovered in a play titled *Mostellaria.*

In 1972, Phil Silvers at last got his chance to appear as Pseudolus in a well-received revival whose run was curtailed by the star's illness. Both Mostel (as Pseudolus) and Silvers (as Marcus Lycus) were in the 1966 United Artists screen version, along with Jack Gilford and Buster Keaton. Richard Lester was the director.

HAPPY END

MUSIC: Kurt Weill
WORDS: Bertolt Brecht
ADAPTATION: Elisabeth Hauptmann
OPENED: 9/2/29 (Berlin)

Few musical plays have fostered such high expectations and received such complete condemnation as did *Happy End* at the time of its premiere. The German press seemed convinced that Brecht and Weill had attempted to duplicate their early success with *The Threepenny Opera,* and the virtually unanimous verdict was that they had failed miserably. It was not until the 1956 revival in Munich that the show began to be seen and appreciated on its own terms. *Happy End* seems to be slowly gaining a following, yet still remains one of Weill's least known works. The one song from the show which has always maintained a fame of its own, even among the infamy of the show's premiere, is "Surabaya Johnny." It is sung by Lilian Holiday, lieutenant of the Salvation Army, to Bill Cracker, a Chicago gangster and dance hall owner. Lilian chose this song to sing to Bill because she is out to save his soul, as well as trying to convince him of the pain he has caused her.

THE KING AND I

MUSIC: Richard Rodgers   **CHOREOGRAPHER:** Jerome Robbins
LYRICS AND BOOK: Oscar Hammerstein II
DIRECTOR: John van Druten
OPENED: 3/29/51

The idea of turning Margaret Landon's Novel, Anna And The King Of Siam, into a musical first occurred to Gertrude Lawrence who saw it as a suitable vehicle for her return to the Broadway musical stage. Based on the diaries of an adventurous Englishwoman, the story is set in Bangkok in the early 1860s. Anna Leonowens, who has accepted the post of schoolteacher to the Siamese king's children, has frequent clashes with the monarch but eventually comes to exert great influence on him, particularly in creating a more democratic society for his people. The show marked the fifth collaboration between Richard Rodgers and Oscar Hammerstein II, and their third to run over one thousand performances.

Cast opposite Miss Lawrence (who died in 1952 during the run of the play) was the little-known Yul Brynner. After the original production, Brynner virtually made the King his personal property. In 1956, he co-starred with Deborah Kerr in the Fox movie version directed by Walter Lang. Twenty years later, by now solo starred, he began touring in a new stage production which played New York in 1977 with Constance Towers as Anna, and London in 1979 with Virginia McKenna as Anna. Brynner resumed touring in 1981 and, at the time of his death in 1985, had given thousands of performances as King Rama IV.

KISS ME, KATE

MUSIC AND LYRICS: Cole Porter
DIRECTOR: John C. Wilson
OPENED: 12/30/48

BOOK: Samuel and Bella Spewack
CHOREOGRAPHER: Hanya Holm

The genesis of Cole Porter's longest-running musical occurred in 1935 when producer Saint Subber, then a stagehand for the Theatre Guild's production of Shakespeare's *Taming Of The Shrew,* became aware that its stars Alfred Lunt and Lynn Fontanne, quarreled almost as much in private as did the characters in the play. Years later he offered this parallel story as the basis for a musical comedy to the same writing trio, Porter and the Spewacks, who had already worked on the successful show, *Leave It To Me!* The entire action of *Kiss Me, Kate* occurs backstage and onstage at Ford's Theatre, Baltimore, during a tryout of a musical version of *The Taming Of The Shrew.* The main plot concerns the egotistical actor-producer Fred Graham (Alfred Drake) and his temperamental ex-wife Lili Vanessi (Patricia Morison) who — like Shakespeare's Petruchio and Kate — fight and make up and eventually demonstrate their enduring affection for each other.

One of the chief features of the score is the skillful way Cole Porter combined his own musical world (in "So In Love," "Too Darn Hot," and "Why Can't You Behave?") with Shakespeare's world ("I Hate Men"), while also tossing off a Viennese waltz parody ("Wunderbar") and a comic view of the Bard's plays ("Brush Up Your Shakespeare").

MGM's 1953 screen version, under Geroge Sidney's direction, had a cast headed by Howard Keel, Kathryn Grayson, and Ann Miller.

LADY IN THE DARK

MUSIC: Kurt Weill
LYRICS: Ira Gershwin
DIRECTORS: Hassard Short and Moss Hart
OPENED: 1/23/41

BOOK: Moss Hart
CHOREOGRAPHER: Albertina Rasch

Although dreams had long been employed as a theatrical device, Moss Hart was the first to write a musical play dealing with their psychoanalytic implications. An austere and businesslike Liza Elliot (Gertrude Lawrence), editor of a successful fashion magazine, has been bothered by her dreams and visits a psychoanalyst. Her four haunting dreams revolve around four men: Kendall Nesbitt (Bert Lytell), her married lover who aided her rise to editor; Randy Curtis (Victor Mature), a glamorous but shallow Hollywood star; Russell Paxton (Danny Kaye), the magazine's effeminate and zany photographer; and most importantly, Charlie Johnson (MacDonald Carey), the magazine's crusty advertising manager. In relating her dreams, Liza finally comes to understand that all her decisions in life were made because of her father's rejection. With the exception of "My Ship," the musical numbers were sung only during the elaborate dream sequences Liza describes to her doctor.

Ginger Rogers and Ray Milland starred in the 1944 Paramount film version under the director of Mitchell Leisen.

ME AND JULIET

MUSIC: Richard Rodgers
LYRICS AND BOOK: Oscar Hammerstein II
DIRECTOR: George Abbott
OPENED: 5/28/53

CHOREOGRAPHER: Robert Alton

Me And Juliet was Rodgers and Hammerstein's Valentine to show business, with its action — in *Kiss Me, Kate* fashion — taking place both backstage in a theatre and onstage during the performance of a play. Here the tale concerns a romance between a singer in the chorus (Isabel Bigley) and the assistant stage manager (Bill Hayes) whose newfound bliss is seriously threatened by the jealous electrician (Mark Dawson). A comic romantic subplot involves the stage manager (Ray Walston) and the principal dancer (Joan McCracken). The melody of the show's best-remembered song, "No Other Love," had previously been composed by Rodgers as background music for the "Beneath the Southern Cross" episode in the NBC-TV documentary series, *Victory At Sea.*

MERRILY WE ROLL ALONG

MUSIC AND LYRICS: Stephen Sondheim
DIRECTOR: Harold Prince
OPENED: 11/16/81

BOOK: George Furth
CHOREOGRAPHER: Larry Fuller

Founded on the George S. Kaufman-Moss Hart play of the same name, *Merrily We Roll Along* had a highly innovative concept: it told its tale backwards — or from the present when Franklin Shepard (Jim Walton) is a rich, famous, but morally compromised film producer and composer to his idealistic youth when he graduated from high school. Though daring and original, *Merrily We Roll Along* proved too much of a musical morality play, and represented the only out-and-out commercial failure with which composer-lyricist Sondheim and director Prince were associated together.

THE MOST HAPPY FELLA

MUSIC, LYRICS AND BOOK: Frank Loesser   **CHOREOGRAPHER:** Dania Krupska
DIRECTOR: Joseph Anthony
OPENED: 5/3/56

Adapted from Sidney Howard's Pulitzer Prize-winning play, *They Knew What They Wanted, The Most Happy Fella* was a particularly ambitious work for the Broadway theatre, with more than thirty separate musical numbers including arias, duets, trios, quartets, choral pieces, and recitatives. Robust, emotional expressions (such as "Joey, Joey, Joey") were interspersed with more traditional specialty numbers (such as "Big 'D'" and "Standing On The Corner"), though in the manner of an opera, the program credits did not list individual selections. In the story, set in California's Napa Valley, an aging vinyard owner (played by opera singer Robert Weede, in his first Broadway role) proposes to a waitress, Rosabella (Jo Sullivan), by mail and she accepts. Rosabella is so upset to find Tony old and fat that, on their wedding night, she allows herself to be seduced by Joe, the handsome ranch foreman (Art Lund). Once he discovers that his wife is to have another man's child, Tony threatens to kill Joe, but there is a reconciliation and the vintner even offers to raise the child as his own. A revival of *The Most Happy Fella* played on Broadway in 1979, with Giorgio Tozzi in the leading role. It ran 52 performances.

THE MUSIC MAN

MUSIC, LYRICS AND BOOK: Meredith Willson   **CHOREOGRAPHER:** Onna White
DIRECTOR: Morton Da Costa
OPENED: 12/19/57

With *The Music Man,* composer-lyricist-librettist Meredith Willson recaptured the innocent charm of the middle America he knew growing up in an Iowa town. It is the Fourth of July, 1912, in River City, Iowa, and "Professor" Harold Hill, a traveling salesman of musical instruments, has arrived to con the citizens into believing that he can teach the town's children how to play in a marching band. But instead of skipping town before the instruments are to arrive, Hill is persuaded to remain because of the love of a good woman, librarian Marian Paroo. The story ends with the children, though barely able to produce any kind of a recognizable musical sound, being hailed by their proud parents.

The show, which took eight years and over thirty rewrites before it was produced on Broadway, marked Willson's auspicious debut in the theatre.

It was also the first musical-stage appearance of Robert Preston, playing the role of Harold Hill, who went on to repeat his dynamic performance in the 1962 Warner Bros. screen version. Shirley Jones and Hermione Gingold were also in the movie, which was directed by the original stage director, Morton Da Costa.

MY FAIR LADY

MUSIC: Frederick Loewe   **CHOREOGRAPHER:** Hanya Holm
LYRICS AND BOOK: Alan Jay Lerner
DIRECTOR: Moss Hart
OPENED: 3/15/56

The most celebrated musical of the 1950s began as an idea of Hungarian film producer Garbiel Pascal, who devoted the last two years of his life trying to find writers to adapt George Bernard Shaw's play, *Pygmalion,* into a stage musical. The team of Lerner and Loewe also saw the possibilities, particularly when they realized that they could use most of the original dialogue and simply expand the action to include scenes at the Ascot Races and the Embassy Ball. They were also scrupulous in maintaining the Shavian flavor in their songs, most apparent in such pieces as "Get Me To The Church On Time," "Just you Wait," "Why Can't The English?," "Show Me," and "Without You."

Shaw's concern with class distinction and his belief that barriers would fall if all Englishmen would learn to speak properly was conveyed through a story about Eliza Doolittle (Julie Andrews) a scruffy flower seller in Covent Garden, who takes speech lessons from Prof. Henry Higgins (Rex Harrison) so that she might qualify for the position of a florist in a shop. Eliza succeeds so well that she outgrows her social station and — in a development added by librettist Lerner — even makes Higgins fall in love with her. Though the record was subsequently broken, *My Fair Lady* became the longest running production in Broadway history, remaining for over six and a half years. Two major revivals were mounted in New York. In 1976, the musical ran for 377 performances with Ian Richardson and Christine Andreas as Higgins and Eliza; in 1981, it lasted 119 performances with Rex Harrison in his original role and Nancy Ringham. Harrison and Audrey Hepburn (whose singing was dubbed by Marni Nixon) were costarred in the 1964 Warner Bros. movie version, which was directed by George Cukor.

OKLAHOMA!

MUSIC: Richard Rodgers

CHOREOGRAPHER: Agnes de Mille

LYRICS AND BOOK: Oscar Hammerstein II

DIRECTOR: Rouben Mamoulian

OPENED: 3/31/43

There are many reasons why *Oklahoma!* is a recognized landmark in the history of the American musical theatre. In the initial collaboration between Richard Rodgers and Oscar Hammerstein II, it not only expertly fused the major elements in the production — story, songs and dances — it also utilized dream ballets to reveal hidden desires and fears of the principals. In addition, the musical, based on Lynn Riggs' play, *Green Grow The Lilacs,* was the first with a book that honestly depicted the kind of rugged pioneers who had once tilled the land and tended the cattle. Set in Indian Territory soon after the turn of the century, *Oklahoma!* spins a simple tale mostly concerned with whether the decent Curly (Alfred Drake) or the menacing Jud (Howard Da Silva) gets to take Laurey (Joan Roberts) to the box social. Though she chooses Jud in a fit of pique, Laurey really loves Curly and they soon make plans to marry. At their wedding they join in celebrating Oklahoma's impending statehood, then — after Jud is accidentally killed in a fight with Curly — the couple ride off in their surrey with the fringe on top.

With its Broadway run of five years, nine months, *Oklahoma!* established a long-run record that it held for fifteen years. It also toured the United States and Canada for over a decade. In 1979, the musical was revived on Broadway with a cast headed by Laurence Guittard and Christine Andreas, and ran for 293 performances. The film version, the first in Todd-AO, was released by Magna in 1955. Gordon MacRae, Shirley Jones and Charlotte Greenwood were in it, and the director was Fred Zinnemann.

110 IN THE SHADE

MUSIC: Harvey Schmidt

LYRICS: Tom Jones

BOOK: N. Richard Nash

CHOREOGRAPHER: Agnes de Mille

DIRECTOR: Joseph Anthony

OPENED: 10/24/63

N. Richard Nash adapted his own play, *The Rainmaker,* for Schmidt and Jones' first Broadway musical, following their wildly successful *The Fantasticks* Off-Broadway. Nash's play is probably best remembered for the film version which starred Burt Lancaster and Katharine Hepburn. The plot of the musical version remains quite faithful to that of its predecessor. It is a simple tale of Lizzie, an aging unmarried woman who lives with her father and brothers on a drought-stricken ranch in the American west. Starbuck, a transient "rainmaker" comes on the scene and is soon seen to be the con man that he is, despite his dazzling charisma. He does, however, pay sincere attention to Lizzie, and awakens love and life in her. The song in this volume, "Old Maid" is a moving aria that ends the first act, in which Lizzie nakedly reveals her fears of forever being alone.

PORGY AND BESS

MUSIC: George Gershwin

LYRICS: Ira Gershwin and DuBose Heyward

LIBRETTO: DuBose Heyward

DIRECTOR: Rouben Mamoulian

OPENED: 10/10/35

Universally recognized as the most esteemed and popular opera written by an American composer, *Porgy and Bess* began in 1925 as a novel called <u>Porgy</u> by DuBose Heyward. Heyward's setting of Catfish Row in Charleston, South Carolina, and his emotional story of the crippled beggar Porgy, the seductive Bess, the menacing Crown, and the slinky cocaine dealer, Sportin' Life, fired Gershwin's imagination even before Heyward and his wife, Dorothy, transformed the book into a play two years later. After many delays, Gershwin, with Heyward and the composer's brother, Ira, began writing the opera late in 1933, and completed it — including orchestrations — in twenty months.

The initial Broadway production, with Todd Duncan and Anne Brown in the title roles, was not a commercial success, though many of the solos and duets — "Summertime," "Bess, You Is My Woman Now," "I Got Plenty O' Nuttin'," "It Ain't Necessarily So" for example — quickly caught on. Four major revivals of *Porgy and Bess* have been mounted on Broadway since the first engagement. In 1942, again with Todd Duncan and Anne Brown, it ran 286 performances in a somewhat trimmed down version. In 1952, as part of a four-year international tour, it returned with William Warfield and Leontyne Price and ran for 305 performances. An acclaimed production in 1976 by the Houston Grand Opera Company featured Donnie Ray Albert as Porgy and Clamma Dale as Bess, and had a 122-performance run on Broadway. A 1983 production was based on the 1976 version and was the first dramatic work ever staged at the Radio City Music Hall. It gave 45 performances. The Metropolitan Opera produced the work in 1985, the first performances ever given in that house.

ROBERTA

MUSIC: Jerome Kern
LYRICS AND BOOK: Otto Harbach
DIRECTOR: Hassard Short
OPENED: 11/18/33

CHOREOGRAPHER: Jose Limon

The musical was adapted from Alice Duer Miller's novel Gowns by Roberta, but in the end the little plot that remained in the show seems to be a scant framework for some first rate songs. *Roberta* is probably best remembered as the source for its most famous song, "Smoke Gets In Your Eyes," which appears in this volume. Two film versions were made of the play, the first one in 1935 and starring Irene Dunne, Fred Astaire and Ginger Rogers.

SHOW BOAT

MUSIC: Jerome Kern
LYRICS AND BOOK: Oscar Hammerstein II
DIRECTOR: Zeke Colvan
OPENED: 12/27/27

CHOREOGRAPHER: Sammy Lee

No show ever to hit Broadway was more historically important, and at the same time more beloved than *Show Boat,* that landmark of the 1927 season. Edna Ferber's novel of life on the Mississippi was the source for this musical/operetta, and provided a rich plot and characters which Kern and Hammerstein amplified to become some of the most memorable ever to grace the stage. *Show Boat* is not only a summing up of all that had come before it, both in the musical and operetta genres, but plants a seed of complete congruity which later further blossoms in the more adventurous shows of the '30's, '40's and '50's. Almost every song in the show is a familiar gem: "Make Believe"; "Can't Help Lovin' Dat Man"; "You Are Love"; "Why Do I Love You?"; "Bill"; and that most classic song of the musical stage, "Ol' Man River." Since its premiere in 1927 the show has been in constant revival in some way or another, whether in its three film versions, in New York productions, in touring companies, in operatic repertories, or in the many, many amateur productions. *Show Boat* seems to be a permanent fixture in musical theatre.

THE SOUND OF MUSIC

MUSIC: Richard Rodgers
DIRECTOR: Vincent J. Donehue
LYRICS: Oscar Hammerstein II
OPENED: 11/16/59

BOOK: Howard Linsay and Russel Crouse
CHOREOGRAPHER: Joe Layton

Rodgers and Hammerstein's final collaboration became their third longest running Broadway production. The story of *The Sound Of Music* was adapted from Maria Von Trapp's autobiographical The Trapp Family Singers and the German film version, which Mary Martin was convinced would provide her with an ideal stage vehicle. Her husband, Richard Halliday, and producer Leland Hayward secured the rights and, initially, they planned to use only the music associated with the famed singing family plus one additional song by Rodgers and Hammerstein. Eventually, the songwriters were asked to contribute the entire score, and they also joined Halliday and Hayward as producers.

The play is set in Austria in 1938, Maria Rainier (Miss Martin), a free-spirited postulant at Nonnburg Abbey, takes a position as governess to the seven children of the widowed and autocratic Capt. Georg Von Trapp (Theodore Bikel). After Maria and the captain fall in love and marry, their happiness is quickly shattered by the Nazi invasion which forces the family to flee over the Alps to Switzerland.

The 1965 film version, presented by 20th Century-Fox and directed by Robert Wise, starred Julie Andrews and Christopher Plummer. According to *Variety,* from 1966 through 1969 *The Sound Of Music* was the All-Time Box-Office Champion in rentals received in the U.S.-Canadian Market.

STREET SCENE

MUSIC: Kurt Weill
LYRICS: Langston Hughes
DIRECTOR: Charles Friedman
OPENED: 1/9/47

BOOK: Elmer Rice
CHOREOGRAPHER: Anna Sokolow

Kurt Weill persuaded Elmer Rice to write the libretto based on his own Pulitzer Prize winning play with poet Langston Hughes supplying the powerful and imaginative lyrics. Billed as "a dramatic musical," the blending of drama and music was very close to genuine opera. In fact, the play went on in 1966 to become part of the repertory of the New York City Opera Company. The story deals principally with the brief, star-crossed romance of Sam Kaplan (Brian Sullivan) and Rose Maurrant (Anne Jeffreys) and the tragic consequences of the infidelity of Rose's mother (Polyna Stoska). This plot loosely frames a series of vignettes, each depicting one of the colorful characters inhabiting the seedy tenement of the setting.

"Somehow I Never Could Believe" is one of the few truly great arias ever to emerge from a Broadway show. It is a full-blown, soaring operatic masterpiece which shows Weill at his American best.

SWEENEY TODD, THE DEMON BARBER OF FLEET STREET

MUSIC AND LYRICS: Stephen Sondheim   **BOOK:** Hugh Wheeler
DIRECTOR: Harold Prince
OPENED: 3/1/79

Despite the sordidness of its main plot — a half-mad, vengeance-obsessed barber in Victorian London slits the throats of his customers whose corpses are then turned into meat pies by his accomplice, Mrs. Lovett — this near-operatic musical was a bold and often brilliant depiction of the cannibalizing effects of the Industrial Revolution. Sweeney Todd first appeared on the London stage in 1842 in a play called *A String Of Pearls, Or The Fiend Of Fleet Street.* Other versions followed, the most recent being Christopher Bond's *Sweeney Todd,* produced in 1973, which served as the basis of the musical. Sondheim's masterwork is quickly gaining a foothold in the operatic repertory, with prominent productions at Houston and at New York City Opera.

THE THREEPENNY OPERA

MUSIC: Kurt Weill
WORDS: Bertolt Brecht
ENGLISH TRANSLATION: Marc Blitzstein
OPENED: 1928 (Berlin), 3/10/54 (New York)

The premiere of *The Threepenny Opera* in 1928 marked the 200th anniversary of *The Beggar's Opera,* and the earlier work is the basis for the famous Brecht-Weill collaboration. It revealed a revolutionary new style of German musical theatre, full of sardonic wit and political power. "Mack the Knife" has proven to be a durably popular product of the show, recorded and performed in widely varying styles and arrangements. Although the show had been performed in New York as early as the '30's, it didn't gain wide popularity until the famous 1954 production which starred Weill's widow, Lotte Lenya. That production went on to boast one of the longest runs in New York theatrical history, and the show continues to frequently appear on stages around the world.

TREEMONISHA

MUSIC AND LIBRETTO: Scott Joplin   **CHOREOGRAPHER:** Louis Johnson
DIRECTOR: Frank Corsaro
OPENED: 10/21/75

Early in the century, the celebrated ragtime composer Scott Joplin took the bold step of creating an opera, *Treemonisha,* but he didn't live to see it performed on the stage. Almost seventy years later, after arranger Gunther Schuller had recreated the score from fragments, the work was given its world premiere by the Houston Grand Opera, which was the same production later shown on Broadway. In the story, set in Arkansas soon after the Civil War, the well-educated Treemonisha (so-named because as a child she was found under a tree) — is abducted by a voodoo conjurer to prevent her from enlightening her superstitious neighbors. Treemonisha is rescued, forgives her abductor, and becomes a leader of her people.

TWO BY TWO

MUSIC: Richard Rodgers   **BOOK:** Peter Stone
LYRICS: Martin Charnin
DIRECTOR: Joe Layton
OPENED: 1/10/70

After an absence of almost thirty years, Danny Kaye returned to Broadway in a musical based on the legend of Noah and the Ark. Adapted from Clifford Odets' play, *The Flowering Peach, Two By Two* dealt primarily with Noah's rejuvenation and his relationship with his wife and family as he undertakes the formidable task that God has commanded. During the run, Kaye suffered a torn ligament in his left leg and was briefly hospitalized. He returned hobbling on a crutch with his leg in a cast, a situation he used as an excuse to depart from the script by cutting up and clowning around. For his third musical following Oscar Hammerstein's death, composer Richard Rodgers joined lyricist Martin Charnin (later to be responsible for *Annie*) to create a melodious score that included "I Do Not Know A Day I Did Not Love You."

COME HOME
from *Allegro*

Music by RICHARD RODGERS
Lyrics by OSCAR HAMMERSTEIN II

lie by a laugh-ing spring ____ Where the breez - es sing, ____

____ And ca - ress your ear.____ There is no

sweet - er sound ____ For a man to hear.____ Come home, Joe, ____

____ come home.____ You will find a world of

hon - est friends who miss you,_____ You will shake the hands of

men whose hands are strong._____ And when all their wives and

kids run up and kiss you,_____ You will know that you are

back where you be - long _____ You'll know you're back where there's

work to do,_____ Where there's love for you _____ For the love you

give. _____ There is no bet-ter life _____ For a man to

live, _____ Come home, Joe, _____ come home,_____

___ Come home, Joe, _____ come home. _____

WHERE OR WHEN
from *Babes In Arms*

Words by LORENZ HART
Music by RICHARD RODGERS

The clothes you're wear-ing are the clothes you wore. The smile you are smil-ing you were smil-ing then, But I can't re-mem-ber where or when. Some things that hap-pen for the first time_____ Seem to be hap-pen-ing a-

Some things that hap - pen for the first time

Seem to be hap - pen - ing a -

gain_____ And so it seems that we have

met be - fore And laughed be - fore And

loved be - fore, But who knows where or

when.

FALLING IN LOVE WITH LOVE

from *The Boys From Syracuse*

Words by LORENZ HART
Music by RICHARD RODGERS

thread, but leave _____ The whole

heart whole. _____

Mer - ry maids can sew and

In 3

sleep, Wives can on - ly sew and weep!

L.H.

rall.

A tempo - In 1

Fall - ing in love with love Is fall - ing for make - be - lieve.

Fall - ing in love with love Is play - ing the

fool. Car - ing too much is

such a ju - ve - nile fan - cy.

Learn- ing to trust is just for chil - dren in school. _____

I fell in love with love One night when the

moon was full. _____ I was un - wise with

eyes Un - a - ble to see. _____

cresc. poco a poco

In 3

A shade slower

I fell in love with love One night when the moon was full._____ I was un-wise with eyes Un-a-ble to see._____

rall. espress. mp p

cresc. poco a poco

I LOVED YOU ONCE IN SILENCE
from *Camelot*

Words by ALAN JAY LERNER
Music by FREDERICK LOEWE

All the while not know - ing You loved me too.

Yes, loved me in lone - some si - lence;

Your heart filled with dark des - pair... Think-ing

love would flame in you for - ev - er, And I'd nev - er,

(Mosso)

nev - er know the flame was there._____ Then one

day we cast a - way our se - cret long - ing;_____ The rag - ing

(Tempo I)

tide we held in - side would hold no more._____ The si - lence_____

dolce

_____ at last was bro - ken!_____ We flung wide_____ our pris - on

34

THE SIMPLE JOYS OF MAIDENHOOD
from *Camelot*

Words by ALAN JAY LERNER
Music by FREDERICK LOEWE

Animato molto

Moderato

GUENEVERE:

St. Gen-e-vieve! St. Gen-e-vieve! It's

Guen-e-vere! Re-mem-ber me? St. Gen-e-vieve! St. Gen-e-vieve! I'm

o-ver here be-neath this tree. You know how faith-ful and de-vout I am. You

must ad-mit I've al-ways been a lamb. But Gen-e-vieve, St. Gen-e-vieve, I

Moderato
(*plaintively*)

Oh, Gen - e - vieve, St. Gen - e - vieve, Where were you when my youth was sold? Dear

Gen - e - vieve, sweet Gen - e - vieve, Shan't I be young be - fore I'm

Allegro   *Optional cut to* **✶✶**

old?

**If the cut is taken the spoken lines are omitted.

Allegretto
(She sings)

Where are the sim-ple joys of maid-en-hood?___ Where are

all those a-dor-ing, dar-ing boys?_____ Where's the

knight pin-ing so for me He leaps to death in woe for me? Oh,

where are a maid-en's sim-ple joys?_____ Shan't

I have the nor-mal life a maid-en should?____ Shall I

nev - er be res-cued in the wood?_____ Shall two

knights nev - er tilt for me And let their blood be spilt for me? Oh,

where are the sim-ple joys of maid - en - hood?

IF I LOVED YOU
from *Carousel*

Words by OSCAR HAMMERSTEIN II
Music by RICHARD RODGERS

MISTER SNOW
from *Carousel*

Music by RICHARD RODGERS
Music by OSCAR HAMMERSTEIN II

you'll be mine, I'll be yours fer the rest of my life!" Next

mo - ment we were prom- ised! And now my mind's in a

maze, Fer all it ken do is look for - ward to That

won - der - ful day of days.

REFRAIN

Moderato *(with expression)*

When I mar - ry Mis - ter Snow,

The flow-ers 'll be buz-zin' with the hum of bees, The

birds 'll make a rack-et in the church - yard trees, When I

mar - ry Mis - ter Snow.

lamb. Then he'll set me on my feet And I'll say, kind a sweet,

"Well, Mis - ter Snow,— here I am!" Then I'll

kiss him so he'll know That

ev - 'ry - thin' 'll be as right as right ken be, A-

liv - in' in a cot - tage by the sea with me, For I

love that Mis - ter Snow,_____ That young, sea - far - in',

bold and dar - in', Big, be - whis - kered, o - ver bear - in'

dar - lin', Mis - ter Snow!_____

WHAT'S THE USE OF WOND'RIN'
from *Carousel*

Music by RICHARD RODGERS
Lyrics by OSCAR HAMMERSTEIN II

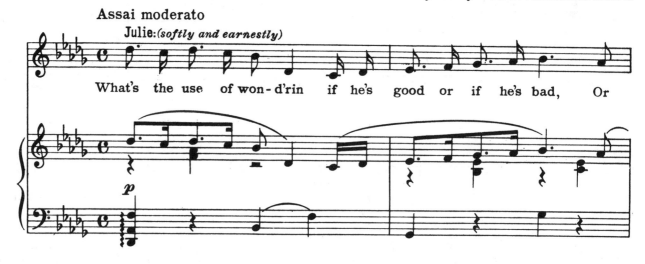

that._____ Com-mon sense may tell you, That the

end - in' will be sad, And now's the time to break and run a -

way. But what's the use of won-d'rin' if the end - in' will be sad? He's your

fel - ler and you love him— There's noth-in more to say._____

Some-thin' made him the way that he is, ___

Wheth-er he's false___ or true And some-thin' gave him the

things that are his ___ One of those things is you. So

when he wants your kiss - es you will give them to the lad, And

an - y-where he leads you, you will walk and an - y-time he needs you, you'll go

run - nin' there like mad! You're his girl and he's your fel - ler

And all the rest is "talk!"

YOU'LL NEVER WALK ALONE
from *Carousel*

Words by OSCAR HAMMERSTEIN II
Music by RICHARD RODGERS

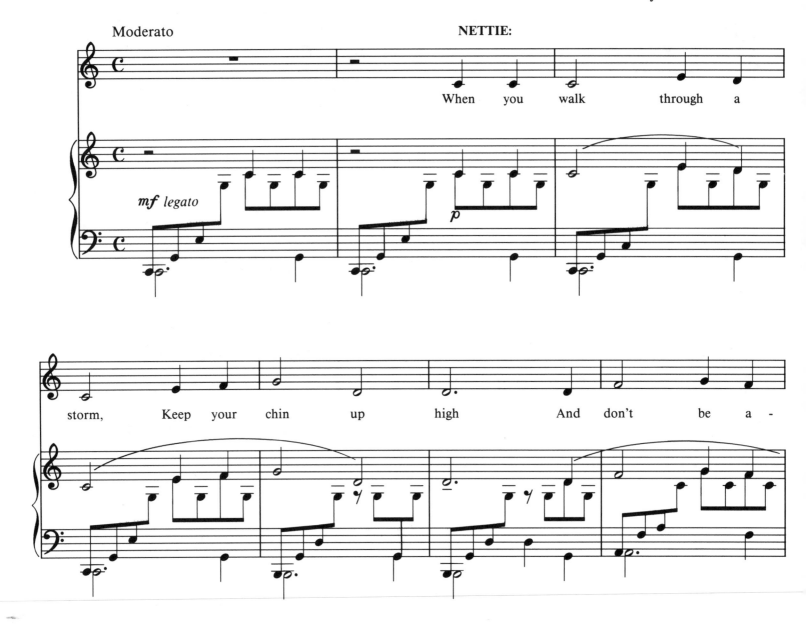

UNDER THE TREE
from *Celebration*

Lyrics by TOM JONES
Music by HARVEY SCHMIDT

This song was originally written for a solo singer with a trio as a chorus.

Die and I think I would die.
Grieve and my own heart starts

griev - ing.
You and I we are one per - son.

Flesh of my flesh God made you.
Part of my own in -

side.
And we must stay for - ev - er,

I HAVE TO TELL YOU
from *Fanny*

Music and Lyrics by
HAROLD ROME

MUCH MORE
from *The Fantasticks*

Words by TOM JONES
Music by HARVEY SCHMIDT

*small notes are optional throughout.

FAR FROM THE HOME I LOVE

from *Fiddler On The Roof*

Lyrics by SHELDON HARNICK
Music by JERRY BOCK

Andantino - in 4

In 2

HODEL:
How can I hope to make you un - der - stand Why I do what I do?

Why I must trav - el to a dis - tant land, Far from the home I love.

Once I was hap - pi - ly con - tent to be As I was, Where I was;

Clos - ing my heart to ev-'ry hope but his; Leav - ing the home I love.

There where my heart has set -tled long a - go. I must go I must go.

In 4

Who could im - ag - ine I'd be wand - 'ring so Far from the home I

love. Yet there with my love I'm home.

rall.

pp rit.

p

LOVE, LOOK AWAY
from *Flower Drum Song*

Words by OSCAR HAMMERSTEIN II
Music by RICHARD RODGERS

ONE MORE KISS
from *Follies*

Music and Lyrics by
STEPHEN SONDHEIM

A Slow Waltz

HEIDI:

One more kiss be-fore we part,—

One more kiss and fare-well.

Nev - er —— shall we meet a - gain, —— Just a kiss and then we

In the show this song is sung as a duet (two sopranos).

THAT'LL SHOW HIM
from *A Funny Thing Happened On The Way To The Forum*

Words and Music by
STEPHEN SONDHEIM

Our re - venge will start! _____

When I kiss him, I'll be kiss - ing you.

So I'll kiss him morn-ing and night... That -'ll show him!

When I hold him, I'll be hold - ing you,

tent for two, I'll sit on his knee, — Get to know him in - ti - mate - ly, — That - 'll show him How much I real - ly love you!

SURABAYA JOHNNY
from *Happy End*

English words by MICHAEL FEINGOLD
Original German words by BERT BRECHT
Music by KURT WEILL

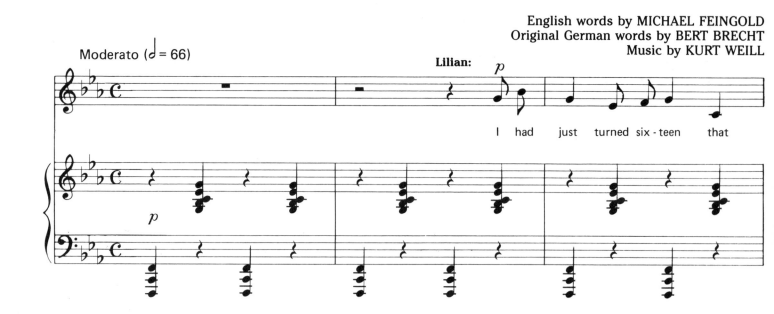

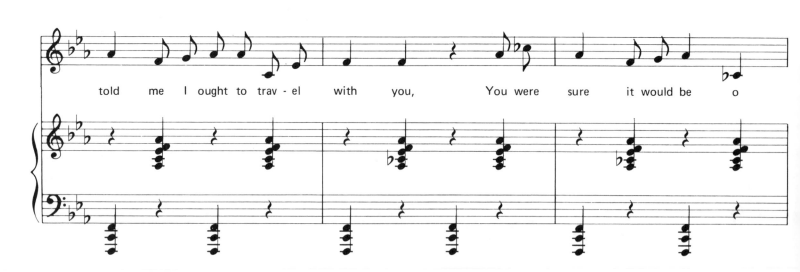

why'm I feel-ing so blue? You have no heart, John-ny,

and I still love you so! At the start ev'-ry day was

Sun-day, till we went on our way one fine night. And be-fore two more weeks were

o-ver you thought noth-ing I did was right. So we trekked up and down through the

pipe out of your mouth, you rat! Su - ra - ba - ya John - ny, no one's

mean - er than you. Su - ra - ba - ya John - ny, (spoken) my God, and

I still love you so! Su - ra - ba - ya John - ny, why'm I

feel - ing so blue? You have no heart, John - ny, and I still love you

ship wait-ing down at the quay.* You have no heart, John-ny, you're just a

louse, John-ny. How can you go, John-ny, and leave me flat? You're still my

love, John - ny, like the day we met, John - ny. *(spoken) Take that damn*

pipe out of your mouth, you rat! Su - ra - ba - ya John - ny,

legato

*pronounced "key"

HELLO, YOUNG LOVERS
from *The King and I*

Words by OSCAR HAMMERSTEIN II
Music by RICHARD RODGERS

ANNA:

Andante con moto ♩ = 84

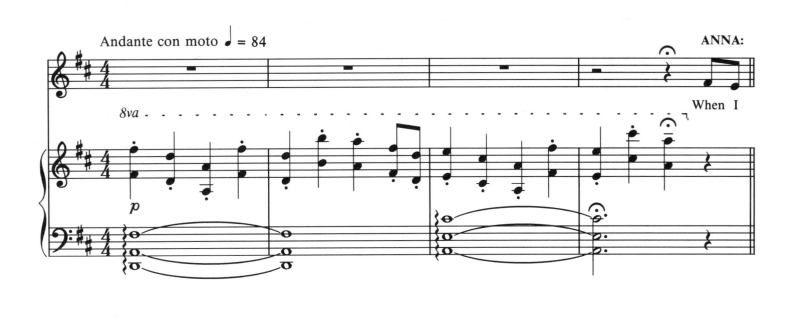

you._____ I know how it feels to have wings on your

heels And to fly down a street in a trance._____ You

fly down a street on the chance that you'll meet, And you meet not

real - ly by chance._____ Don't cry, young lov - ers what -

MY LORD AND MASTER
from *The King And I*

Words by OSCAR HAMMERSTEIN II
Music by RICHARD RODGERS

SOMETHING WONDERFUL
from *The King And I*

Lyrics by OSCAR HAMMERSTEIN II
Music by RICHARD RODGERS

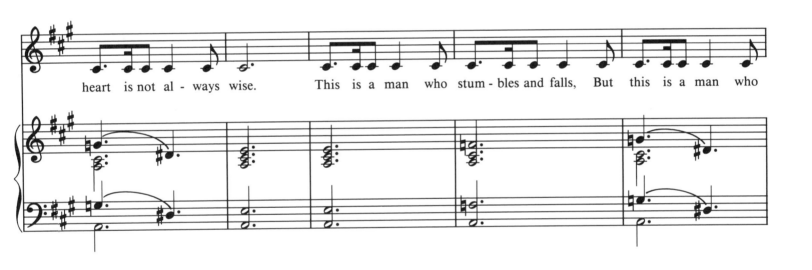

SO IN LOVE
from *Kiss Me, Kate*

Words and Music by
COLE PORTER

LILLI:

Strange, dear, ___ but true dear, ___ When I'm close ___ to you, dear, ___ The stars fill the sky, ___ So in love with you am I. ___

NO OTHER LOVE
from *Me And Juliet*

Words by OSCAR HAMMERSTEIN II
Music by RICHARD RODGERS

free _____ from long - ing. In - to your arms I'll fly. ___

Locked in your arms I'll stay, ___

Wait - ing to hear you say: ___ No oth - er love have

I, No oth - er love. _____

MY SHIP
from *Lady In The Dark*

Words by IRA GERSHWIN
Music by KURT WEILL

NOT A DAY GOES BY
from *Merrily We Roll Along*

Words and Music by
STEPHEN SONDHEIM

SOMEBODY, SOMEWHERE
from *The Most Happy Fella*

By FRANK LOESSER

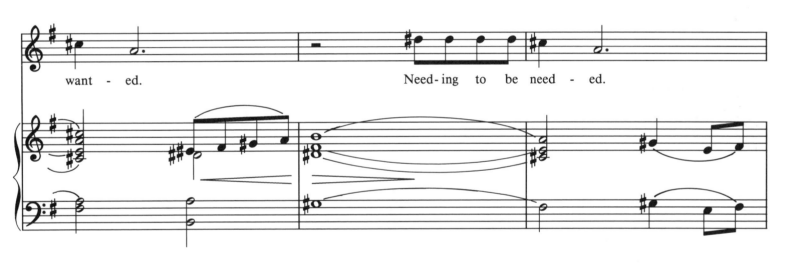

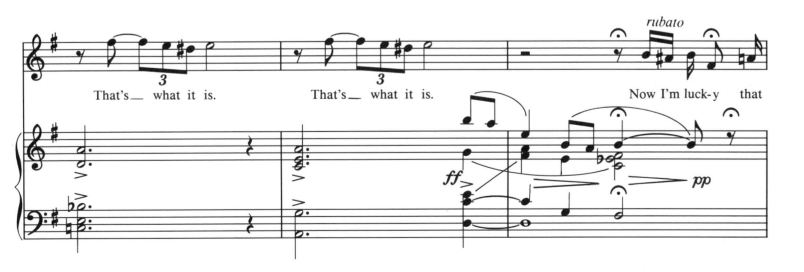

GOODNIGHT, MY SOMEONE
from *The Music Man*

By MEREDITH WILLSON

Poco mosso

True love can be whis-pered from heart to heart, when

lov-ers are part-ed they say. _____ But I must de-

poco rit.

pend on a wish and a star, as long as my heart does-n't

Tempo I

know who you are. Sweet dreams be yours, dear, if dreams there

MY WHITE KNIGHT
from *The Music Man*

By MEREDITH WILLSON

MARIAN: Moderato

My white knight,— not a Lanc-e-lot,— nor an

an-gel with wings; Just some-one to love me,— who is —not a-shamed of a

few nice things. My white knight— what my heart would say if it on-ly knew how.

Slightly slower

Please, dear Ve-nus, show me now.

self. And more in-t'rest-ed in us than in me.

Poco lento

And if oc-ca-sion-'ly he'd pon - der what makes Shakes-peare and Beet-hov-en great,

Lento   **Molto lento**

him I could love 'til I die. Him I could love 'til I die.

Tempo I

My white knight,— not a Lanc-e-lot— nor an an-gel with wings.

Just some-one to love me,— who is not a-shamed of a few nice things.

My white knight,— let me walk with him where the oth-ers ride by;

Walk, and love him— 'til I die. 'Til I

Very broadly

Molto lento

poco cresc.

f

Tempo I

Ossia

die.____

molto cresc.

ff

sfz

TILL THERE WAS YOU
from *The Music Man*

By MEREDITH WILLSON

MARIAN: Moderato e Rubato

There were bells on the hill, but I

nev - er heard them ring - ing. No, I nev - er heard them at all, till there was

you. _____ There were birds in the sky, but I nev - er saw them wing - ing. No I nev - er saw them at all, till there was you. _____ And there was mu - sic and there were won - der - ful ro - ses, they tell me, in sweet frag - rant mea - dows of

R.H.

L.H. col voce

R.H.

dawn and dew. There was love all a-round, but I

nev-er heard it sing-ing. No, I nev-er heard it at all, till there was

you.

R.H.

p

mp   *mf*

sempre cresc.

f   *cresc. molto*

There was love all a-round, but I nev-er heard it sing-ing. No, I nev-er heard it at all, till there was you.

I COULD HAVE DANCED ALL NIGHT
from *My Fair Lady*

Words by ALAN JAY LERNER
Music by FREDERICK LOEWE

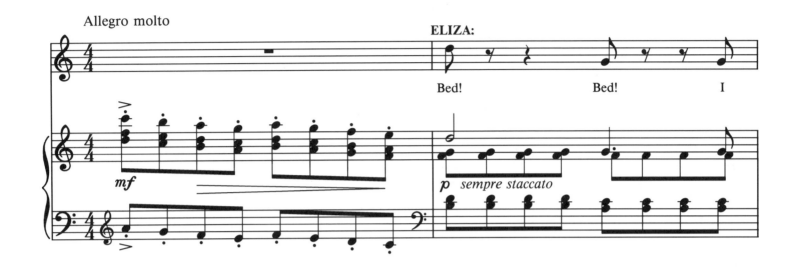

could - n't sleep to - night! Not for all the

jew - els in the crown! I could have

danced all night! I could have danced all

night! And still have begged for

SHOW ME
from *My Fair Lady*

Words by ALAN JAY LERNER
Music by FREDERICK LOEWE

Here we are to-geth-er in the mid-dle of the night! Don't talk of
Nev-er do I ev-er want to hear an-oth-er word. There is - n't

spring! Just hold me tight!
one I have - n't heard.

An - y - one who's ev - er been in love - 'll tell you that
Here we are to-geth-er in what ought to be a dream;

This is no time for a chat!
Say one more time word and I'll scream!

un - dy - ing vow. Show
o - ver my brow. Show

me now.
me

now.

MANY A NEW DAY
from *Oklahoma!*

Words by OSCAR HAMMERSTEIN II
Music by RICHARD RODGERS

LAUREY:

Why should a wo-man who is health-y and strong Blub-ber like a ba-by if her man goes a-way? A-weep-in' and a-wail-in' how he's done her wrong, That's one thing you'll nev-er hear me say! Nev-er gon-na think that the

Nev-er-'ve I once looked back to sigh o-ver the ro - mance be - hind me,

Man-y a new day will dawn be - fore I do!

Man-y a light lad may kiss and fly, A kiss gone by is by - gone,

Nev-er-'ve I asked an Au-gust sky, "Where has last Ju - ly gone?"

Nev- er -'ve I wan - dered through the rye, Won-der- in' where has some

guy gone, Man-y a new day will dawn be - fore I do!

Nev-er-'ve I chased the hon- ey bee who care - less - ly ca -

joled me, Some-bod- y else just as sweet as he, cheered me and con -

L.H.

soled me. Nev-er-'ve I wept in - to my tea o - ver the deal some - one

doled me, Man-y a new day will dawn, Man-y a red sun will

poco rit.

set, Man-y a blue moon will shine, be - fore I

rit.

do!

f a tempo

OUT OF MY DREAMS
from *Oklahoma!*

Words by OSCAR HAMMERSTEIN II
Music by RICHARD RODGERS

Tempo di valse

This song appears in a somewhat different form here than in the context of the show.
Mr. Hammerstein revised the lyrics so that the song could stand alone, and it is this revision that is used here.

dreams and in-to the hush of fall - ing shad -

ows, When the mist is low_____ and stars are

break - ing through._____ Then out of my dreams I'll go_____

_____ In - to a dream_____ with

you.

Won't have to make up an - y more sto - ries

mf

You'll be there! Think of the bright

mid - sum - mer night glo - ries we can

share. _____ Won't have to go on kiss-ing a day -

dream I'll have you _____ You'll

be real _____ Real as the white moon light-ing the

blue. _____ Out of my

poco rit. *p a tempo*

OLD MAID
from *110 In The Shade*

Words by TOM JONES
Music by HARVEY SCHMIDT

mock - ing - bird And lock him in a cage. Vis - it - ing your

kin Year - ly fam - 'ly tours. Must - n't love the

(Spoken)

kids too much. They're nev - er real - ly yours. Old maid!

(Sung)

Old maid! Be kind to your poor aunt

165

(Sung)

all tied up! My clothes seem to be on fi - re!___ They're

ty - ing me up and Burn - ing me to the bone!_____

Why won't it rain?_____

Please let it rain!_____

SUMMERTIME
from *Porgy And Bess*

Words by DUBOSE HEYWARD
Music by GEORGE GERSHWIN

Allegretto semplice

Moderato

170

SMOKE GETS IN YOUR EYES
from *Roberta*

Words by OTTO HARBACH
Music by JEROME KERN

find   All who love are   blind,   When your heart's on

fire,   You must re - a - lise   Smoke gets   in   your   eyes."

So   I   chaffed ___ them and   I   gai - ly laughed ___ to think they could

doubt   my   love.   Yet, to- day ___ my love has flown a- way ___ I am with-

love,
Yet to-day___ my love has flown a-way___ I am with-

out my love.
Now laugh-ing friends de-

ridè Tears I can-not hide,_____
So I smile and

say, "When a love-ly flame dies, Smoke gets in your eyes."_____

BILL
from *Show Boat*

Words by P.G. WODEHOUSE and OSCAR HAMMERSTEIN II
Music by JEROME KERN

CAN'T HELP LOVIN' DAT MAN

from *Show Boat*

Words by OSCAR HAMMERSTEIN II
Music by JEROME KERN

182

CLIMB EV'RY MOUNTAIN
from *The Sound Of Music*

Words by OSCAR HAMMERSTEIN II
Music by RICHARD RODGERS

SOMEHOW I NEVER COULD BELIEVE
from *Street Scene*

Words by LANGSTON HUGHES
Music by KURT WEILL

So I went wan-d'ring down the pave-ments of New

York

And through the sub-way's

roar-ing tun-nels un-der - ground,

Hop - ing I'd dis-cov-er some won - der-ful

poco rall. *p*

love turn out that way? Should love turn out that

Allegretto

p (freely)

way? But then the ba-bies came.

col canto

pizz.

Their lit-tle arms made a ring-a-round-a ro-sy-a-bout me,___

Yet as they grew old - er, they, too, seemed to grow a - way Un-

til e-ven Wil-lie, my lit-tle boy Wil-lie seems he can get a - long_____ with-

Lento, quasi misterioso (♩ = 62)

out me._____ I don't know_____ it looks like something aw-ful hap-pens In the

pizz.

kitch - ens where wo-men wash their dish - es. Days turn to months—months turn to years,

(simile)

The greas-y soap-suds drown our wish-es.

molto cresc. e string.

There's got to be a lit - tle hap - pi - ness some-where ___ some hand to touch ___ that's warm and kind!_____ And there must be two smil - ing eyes some - where

that will smile back in - to mine.

Tempo I

I nev-er could be-lieve_____ that life was meant to

be all dull and grey. I al-ways will be - lieve there'll be a bright-er

day!

WHAT GOOD WOULD THE MOON BE?
from *Street Scene*

Words by LANGSTON HUGHES
Music by KURT WEILL

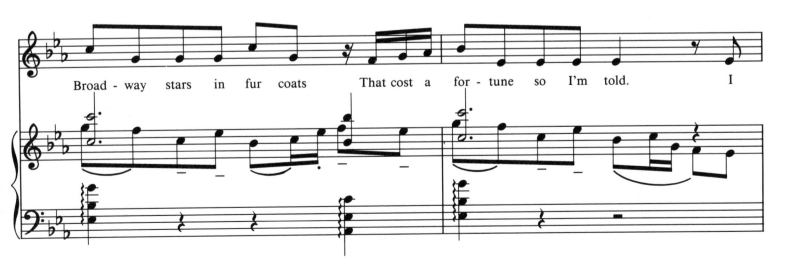

night be _____ Un - less the right lips whis - per

low: Kiss me, oh, dar - ling, kiss me, _____ While ev' - ning

stars still glow? _____ No, it won't be a prim - rose path for ___

molto espr.

me, No, it won't be dia - monds or gold, But may - be there

mf

mf

will be _____ Some - one who'll

love me, _____ Some one who'll

love just me To have and to

hold! _____

L.H.

GREEN FINCH AND LINNET BIRD

from *Sweeney Todd*

Music and Lyrics by
STEPHEN SONDHEIM

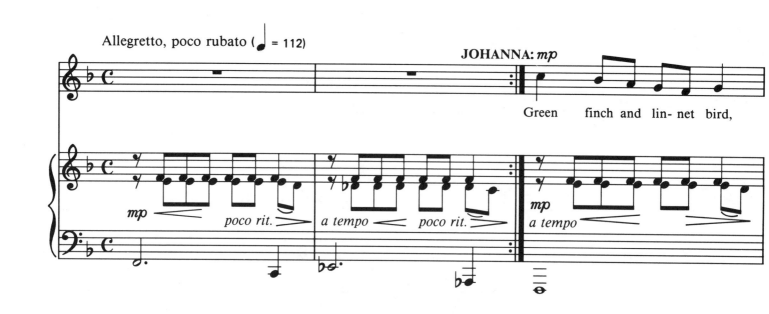

BARBARA SONG
from *The Threepenny Opera*

English Words by MARC BLITZSTEIN
Original German Words by BERT BRECHT
Music by KURT WEILL

good man, if he's a rich man, wears a fine cra - vat,— smokes a ci-
rich men, they were all fine men, wore silk cra - vats— smoked a big ci-
lean man, he was a mean man. He did-n't own a cra-vat,— smoked no ci-

gar, and if he's gal - lant and treats me like a la - dy, then
gar, and since they al-ways made me feel a per-fect la - dy, I
gar, and God knows he nev - er made me feel a la - dy, there

Piu Animato

I shall tell him: "Sor - ry."
said po - lite - ly: "Sor - ry."
just was-n't time for: "Sor - ry."

Chin up high, keep your
I would sigh, keep my
Chin up high? My chin was

poco rit.   *accel.*   *f*

pow - der dry, don't re - lax or go too far.
chin up high, nev - er re - laxed or went too far.
down my shoes, and I re - laxed, but far too far.

Look, the moon is gon - na shine till dawn.
Well I let the moon go shin - ing on.
Oh, the way the moon kept shin - ing on._____ The

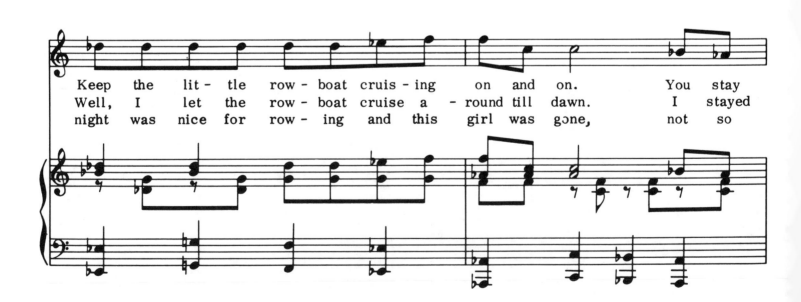

Keep the lit - tle row - boat cruis - ing on and on. You stay
Well, I let the row - boat cruise a - round till dawn. I stayed
night was nice for row - ing and this girl was gone, not so

Broadly

per - pen - di - cu - lar.   Oh,   you   can't   just
per - pen - di - cu - lar.   I   could   not   just
per - pen - di - cu - lar.   So   you   let   a

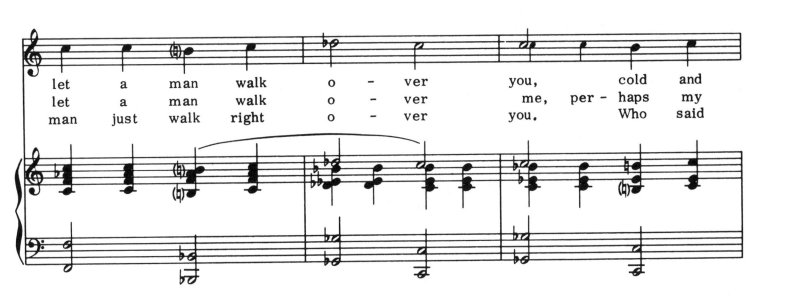

let   a   man   walk   o - ver   you,   cold   and
let   a   man   walk   o - ver   me,   per - haps   my
man   just   walk   right   o - ver   you.   Who   said

dig - ni - fied   is   what   you   are.
dig - ni - ty   went   rath - er   far.
dig - ni - fied   is   what   you   are.

214

PIRATE JENNY
from *The Threepenny Opera*

English Words by MARC BLITZSTEIN
Original German Words by BERT BRECHT
Music by KURT WEILL

makes you feel swell, on a rat - ty wa - ter - front in a
out at the ships; but I'm count - in' your heads while I
down to the ground, on - ly this cheap ho - tel stand - in'

rat - ty old ho - tel, and you nev - er guess to who you're
make up the beds 'cause there's no - bod - y gon - na
up safe and sound, and you yell, "Why the hell spare

talk - in', and you nev - er guess to who you're talk - in'.
sleep here. To - night none of you will sleep here.
that one?" And you yell, "Why the hell spare that one?"

Sud - den - ly one night, there's a scream in the night, and you
Then that night there's a bang in the night, and you
All the night through with the noise and to - do, you

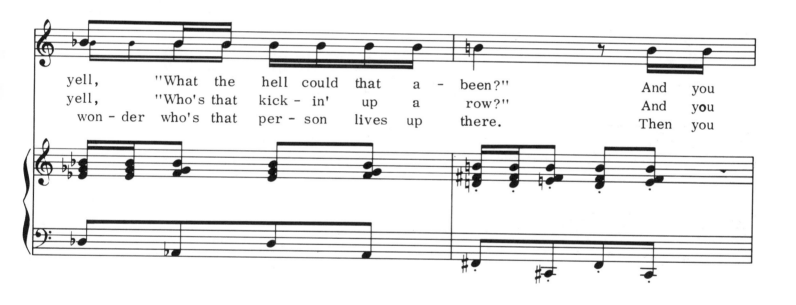

yell, "What the hell could that a - been?" And you
yell, "Who's that kick - in' up a row?" And you
won - der who's that per - son lives up there. Then you

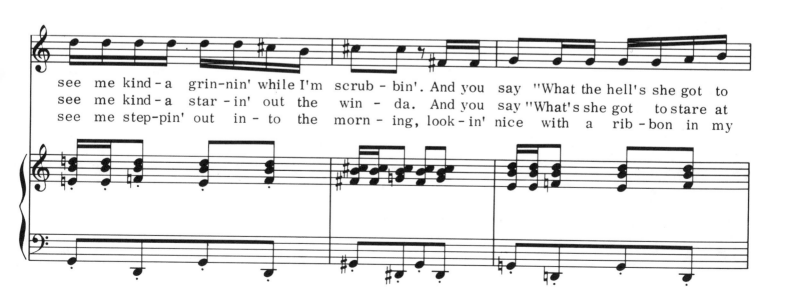

see me kind - a grin-nin' while I'm scrub - bin'. And you say "What the hell's she got to
see me kind - a star - in' out the win - da. And you say "What's she got to stare at
see me step-pin' in - to the morn - ing, look - in' nice with a rib - bon in my

218

hear a fog - horn miles a - way. In that

qui - et of death, I'll say, *(spoken freely)* "Right now!"
And they pile up the bodies and I'll say,

Broadly

p

"That'll learn you!" Then a ship, the black freight - er, dis - ap -

pears out to sea,_____ and on it - is me.

SOLOMON SONG
from *The Threepenny Opera*

English Words by MARC BLITZSTEIN
Original German Words by BERT BRECHT
Music by KURT WEILL

heart, it put him on the spot_____ I was think-ing a-bout____ re-
glam-or put her on the spot._____ I thought____ that glam-or

form -ing,_____ guess not.
paid off,_____ guess not.

Re-mem - ber Jul - ius Cae - sar's

fame____ re - call____ his his - to - ry._____ Of

THE SACRED TREE
from *Treemonisha*

Words and Music by
SCOTT JOPLIN

near that sa - cred tree.

I called to Ned and said,.......... "Wake up, A

ba - by is cry - ing out - side the door."....................... But

Ned said, "You have dreamed e - nough," And went to

sleep once more;............... Yet the ba - by's cry - ing

seemed... to be............ some - where near that...

sa - cred tree, Yet the ba - by's cry - ing

seemed to be some - where near that

very quiet it seemed to be, Some - where

ben marcato

near that sa - cred tree, And ve - ry qui - et it

p

Optional cut from end of bar 106
to beginning of bar 179.

seemed to be,......... Some - where near that sa - cred tree.

cresc.

mp

Ten o'- clock next

p

morn - ing,......... The hot sun......... was shin - ing,......... And the dar - ling lit - tle ba - by......... I real - ly had for - got - ten;......... But I could hear the hum - ming bee,......... Some - where near that sa - cred tree, But I could hear the hum - ming

ba - by's cries.............. And as I list-ened, it seemed to

be, Some - where near that sa - cred tree; And as I

cresc.

f *p a tempo*

Close optional cut.

list - ened, it seemed to be,...... Some - where near that sa - cred

cresc. *mf* *p*

If previous cut is made, use alternate
vocal and text part for bars 184-191.

♩ = 132

tree. Ten I came out in the o' - -

mf *mp*

tree; I found it where I thought 'twould be, There be-

side that sa - cred tree. I

took the child in - to our home, And now the dar - ling girl is

grown, All I've said to you is true, The child I've

The rain or the burn-ing sun, you see,................

Would have sent you to your grave,................ But the sheltering leaves of

that........ old tree,................ Your pre - cious life did save................

.... So now with me............ you must......... a -

gree,............... Not to...... harm that... sa - cred

tree; So now with me you must a

gree, Not to harm that sa - cred

tree.

THE GOLDEN RAM
from *Two By Two*

Words by MARTIN CHARNIN
Music by RICHARD RODGERS

Ye who thirs - teth, Come and drink - eth, The

Gold-en Ram has wa-ters cool and sweet! _____ Ye who

star - veth, Come and sup - peth, The Gold-en Ram is good e-nough to

eat. _____ Huz - zah! _____ Huz - zah! _____

Huz - zah! Huz - zah!

Guess who's got - teth 'em all!

Ye who want - eth, Come and touch - eth, The Gold-en Ram is

vel - vet on thy skin! Ye, who lust - eth,

244

Come and try-eth, The ser-vic-es are wait-ing to be-gin!

Huz - zah! Huz - zah!

Ye who need-eth re - lease! Huz - zah!

Huz - zah! Come and get-teth some

The Singer's Musical Theatre Anthology

SOPRANO

Barbara Song (The Threepenny Opera); Bill (Show Boat); Can't Help Lovin' Dat Man (Show Boat); Climb Ev'ry Mountain (The Sound Of Music); Come Home (Allegro); Falling In Love With Love (The Boys From Syracuse); Far From The Home I Love (Fiddler On The Roof); The Golden Ram (Two By Two); Goodnight, My Someone (The Music Man); Green Finch And Linnet Bird (Sweeney Todd); Hello, Young Lovers (The King And I); I Could Have Danced All Night (My Fair Lady); I Have To Tell You (Fanny); I Loved You Once In Silence (Camelot); If I Loved You (Carousel); Love, Look Away (Flower Drum Song); Many A New Day (Oklahoma!); Mister Snow (Carousel); Much More (The Fantasticks); My Lord And Master (The King And I); My Ship (Lady In The Dark); My White Knight (The Music Man); No Other Love (Me And Juliet); Not A Day Goes By (Merrily We Roll Along); Old Maid (110 In The Shade); One More Kiss (Follies); Out Of My Dreams (Oklahoma!); Pirate Jenny (The Threepenny Opera); The Sacred Tree (Treemonisha); Show Me (My Fair Lady); The Simple Joys Of Maidenhood (Camelot); Smoke Gets In Your Eyes (Roberta); So In Love (Kiss Me, Kate); Solomon Song (The Threepenny Opera); Somebody, Somewhere (The Most Happy Fella); Somehow I Never Could Believe (Street Scene); Something Wonderful (The King And I); Summertime (Porgy And Bess); Surabaya Johnny (Happy End); That'll Show Him (A Funny Thing Happened On The Way To The Forum); Till There Was You (The Music Man); Under The Tree (Celebration); What Good Would The Moon Be? (Street Scene); What's The Use Of Wond'rin' (Carousel); You'll Never Walk Alone (Carousel); Where Or When (Babes In Arms).

MEZZO-SOPRANO/ALTO

Always True To You In My Fashion (Kiss Me, Kate); An Old Man (Two By Two); Anyone Can Whistle (Anyone Can Whistle); Bewitched (Pal Joey); By The Sea (Sweeney Todd); A Cockeyed Optimist (South Pacific); Could I Leave You? (Follies); Do I Hear A Waltz? (Do I Hear A Waltz?); Don't Cry For Me Argentina (Evita); Glad To Be Unhappy (On Your Toes); He Wasn't You (On A Clear Day You Can See Forever); How Are Things In Glocca Mora? (Finian's Rainbow); I Cain't Say No (Oklahoma!); I Love Paris (Can-Can); I'm In Love With A Wonderful Guy (South Pacific); In Buddy's Eyes (Follies); In My Own Little Corner (Cinderella); Just You Wait (My Fair Lady); The Lady Is A Tramp (Babes In Arms); Look To The Rainbow (Finian's Rainbow); Losing My Mind (Follies); Love Song (Celebration); Memory (Cats); The Miller's Son (A Little Night Music); My Favorite Things (The Sound Of Music); My Funny Valentine (Babes In Arms); One Life To Live (Lady In The Dark); People (Funny Girl); The Princess Of Pure Delight (Lady In The Dark); The Saga Of Jenny (Lady In The Dark); Send In The Clowns (A Little Night Music); So Far (Allegro); The Sound Of Music (The Sound Of Music); Stay Well (Lost In The Stars); Trouble Man (Lost In The Stars); Try To Forget (The Cat And The Fiddle); What Did I Have That I Don't Have? (On A Clear Day You Can See Forever); Who Are You Now? (Funny Girl); Why Can't You Behave? (Kiss Me, Kate); The Worst Pies In London (Sweeney Todd).

TENOR

All I Need Is The Girl (Gypsy); All Kinds Of People (Pipe Dream); The Ballad Of Billy M'Caw (Cats); Being Alive (Company); The Big Black Giant (Me And Juliet); The Breeze Kissed Your Hair (The Cat And The Fiddle); Come With Me (The Boys From Syracuse); Fanny (Fanny); Fifty Million Years Ago (Celebration); Finishing The Hat (Sunday In The Park With George); I Am In Love (Can-Can); I Could Write A Book (Pal Joey); I Do Not Know A Day I Did Not Love You (Two By Two); I Talk To The Trees (Paint Your Wagon); If You Could See Her (Cabaret); Kansas City (Oklahoma!); Ladies And Their Sensitivities (Sweeney Todd); The Legend (Song Of Norway); Lonely House (Street Scene); Love, I Hear (A Funny Thing Happened On The Way To The Forum); Make Someone Happy (Do Re Mi); Many Moons Ago (Once Upon A Mattress); A New Love Is Old (The Cat And The Fiddle); Not While I'm Around (Sweeney Todd); On The Street Where You Live (My Fair Lady); The Only Home I Know (Shenandoah); Restless Heart (Fanny); Sitting Pretty (Cabaret); Someone Is Waiting (Company); Stay (Do I Hear A Waltz?); Stranger In Paradise (Kismet); Take The Moment (Do I Hear A Waltz?); That's The Way It Happens (Me And Juliet); When I'm Not Near The Girl I Love (Finian's Rainbow); The Wild Justice (Lost In The Stars); Wish You Were Here (Wish You Were Here); You Are Beautiful (Flower Drum Song); You Are Never Away (Allegro); You've Got To Be Carefully Taught (South Pacific); You Mustn't Kick It Around (Pal Joey); You're Devastating (Roberta); Younger Than Springtime (South Pacific).

BARITONE/BASS

Camelot (Camelot); C'est Moi (Camelot); Come Back To Me (On A Clear Day You Can See Forever); Do I Love You Because You're Beautiful? (Cinderella); Dulcinea (Man Of La Mancha); Everybody Says Don't (Anyone Can Whistle); How To Handle A Woman (Camelot); I Got Plenty O' Nuttin' (Porgy And Bess); I Still See Eliza (Paint Your Wagon); I've Heard It All Before (Shenandoah); If Ever I Would Leave You (Camelot); If I Loved You (Carousel); The Impossible Dream (Man Of La Mancha); Johanna (Sweeney Todd); Lonely Room (Oklahoma!); Lost In The Stars (Lost In The Stars); Mack The Knife (The Threepenny Opera); The Man Of La Mancha (Man Of La Mancha); Meditation I (Shenandoah); Meditation II (Shenandoah); Oh, What A Beautiful Mornin' (Oklahoma!); Ol' Man River (Show Boat); On A Clear Day (On A Clear Day You Can See Forever); A Red Headed Woman (Porgy And Bess); The Road You Didn't Take (Follies); September Song (Knickerbocker Holiday); Soliloquy (Carousel); Some Enchanted Evening (South Pacific); Sorry-Grateful (Company); They Call The Wind Maria (Paint Your Wagon); This Is The Life (Love Life); This Nearly Was Mine (South Pacific); Thousands Of Miles (Lost In The Stars); Try To Remember (The Fantasticks); Wandrin' Star (Paint Your Wagon); Were Thine That Special Face (Kiss Me, Kate); Where Is The Life That Late I Led? (Kiss Me, Kate).

DUETS

Bess, You Is My Woman (Porgy And Bess); I Have Dreamed (The King And I); I Loves You, Porgy (Porgy And Bess); It Never Was You (Knickerbocker Holiday); Make Believe (Show Boat); A Man And A Woman (110 In The Shade); My Heart Is So Full Of You (The Most Happy Fella); People Will Say We're In Love (Oklahoma!); Salzburg (Bells Are Ringing); Strange Music (Song Of Norway); Too Many Mornings (Follies); The Touch Of Your Hand (Roberta); We Kiss In A Shadow (The King And I); We'll Go Away Together (Street Scene); What You Want Wid Bess? (Porgy And Bess); When The Children Are Asleep (Carousel); Will You Remember Me? (Knickerbocker Holiday); With So Little To Be Sure Of (Anyone Can Whistle); Wunderbar (Kiss Me, Kate); You Are Love (Show Boat); You're Nearer (Babes In Arms).